19 Days

My Escape Story

Gitanjali Banik

ISBN
Paperback 979-8-89233-757-1
Hardcase 979-8-89777-381-7

To my dear Arpita, you are missed everyday.

This book is dedicated to my mother. God could not be everywhere so he created mother. My entire journey into medicine started with my mother. Thank you maa for being a part of my journey.

Words will not be enough to thank my dad for sacrificing everything for my education. Thank you babu for letting me be me and standing by me in everything i wanted to do.

To my sisters Pushpa, Hanamoto (pooja), my brother Debabrata.

Thank you Veer, Naren for bringing so much joy

Above all my bestie LK (Lavnya Krishnamurthy) for inspiring me to write my heart out. I can't thank you enough for everything you do for me. It's been 18 years since we both know each other since our college days and nothing has changed. We stay miles apart but still i always feel you are just a phone call away.

Few names i cannot forget in this list Khamba uncle, Chanu Aunty, Soumyadeep, Joydeep and their families. Words are not enough to thank you all for everything you all have done for me. Whatever i am today is all because of you all. Thank you from the bottom of my heart.

Special thank you to Shikha didi, you were not just our help at home but also took care of us like an elder sister.

My thank you list won't end without mentioning the names of "The Retards" … Janaki, Archana, My Roomie Hrudya, Kripa, Meera, Lavnya, Prasanna, Priyanka, Haripriya and their families.

Thank you Partha Sir, Arpita Bhadra Didi.

Thank you Arpita Didi, Jhimli Didi, Mashimoni for being some of the best people i have known in my life. Thank you for the wonderful memories i have spent at your house.

Thank you Sukla Aunty, Ashu Uncle for always being my support system.

Thank you Biswajit, Shubhrajyoti for always being a friend in hard times.

Thank you Augustine for always being there. Thank you Sangeeta.

Thank you to my childhood besties Lopa, Anu, Joyiti for always being there for me.

Thank you Gautami, Deepika, Saroj, Krutika, Alekhya, Anuja, Vijaylashmi for making life little easier during my pg days.

Few people who hold a special place in my life deserve a mention… my dear Mehzabeen, Shreyasi Mukherjee, my big friend Mahantaya, Harika, Lavnya C, Sarfaraz, Anand Venugopal, Chetan, Veerbhadra, Teja, Veeresh, Banasree, Ritu, Moiz, Nilmani, Kumudini mam, Nazima mam.

Thank you to Dr.Pradeep Hopkins for always guiding me like an elder brother.

Thank you to my goodjuniors, seniors who always stood by me.

Thank you to Anjan Kaku.

Thank you to my family.

Thank you to Pooja, Gaurav, Navneet, Rochelle for always being there.

Thank you Sabyasachi.

Thank you to Sujana Mam for being my rock in my toughest times.

Thank you Vanya, Chena, Imlesh for some of the best memories.

The most special person in my life my dadu, Mashi -thank you for everything you have done for us. Although you are not there with us physically dadu, i miss you dadu.

Thank you to my baby sister Komal, Chetan and their family for being there for me always.

Thank you to my good colleagues, teachers.

Thank you Mami, though you are not there physically with us, you are missed everyday.

Thank you to my Alma mater, my good teachers and colleagues.

A special thank you to my brother Gopal for sharing so much in life. Thank you to every kind soul I have met.

Last but not the least thank you to my extended family Janak, Hari G, Arun for always being there for me.

This book is the memoir of a medical aspirant and the hurdles as an entrant. This book should not dishearten anyone who wishes to pursue this journey as a medico. Medicine is still a priced profession and just because of a couple of bad people in the profession no one should think of quitting their dreams of becoming a doctor.

"To all medical aspirants and also aspirants of other branches, medicine or whatever profession you wish for is not the end of life. Life is precious. Sometimes your entire life medical knowledge falls short to save someone's life. Value life. If not medicine there is always a door to other branches. To all parents stand by your children's dream not only in their success but also in their failures."

Contents

Chapter One

Dreams

Like every small town girl, she dreamt of leaving her small town home in her hilly state in a journey she had dreamt of from the time she understood the word "Medicine". She didn't understand the word much as she had no background of introduction into medical field from her non medical family. She just understood the word had a lot of pride and a lot of responsibilities along with it. Now who is she? She is Geet, a medical aspirant who thought this is the world she had dreamt of since the time she understood the importance of Doctors in our everyday life. Her first tryst with medicine came during her sister's multiple hospital admissions for various reasons. As always Geet always ended up being the accompanying person for her sister as her sister didn't want anyone else to be with her during her illness.

As multiple Doctors would come for visits and explain Geet about all the procedures what was done during the surgeries she used to patiently listen to all that was said. She understood very little of what they said but a fascination grew towards the profession. An immense respect grew towards every medical professional and also to all the associated people to this medical field. She just knew one thing this is the only thing she wanted to do in her life and pursue it as a career. She didn't know where to start from but as she neared her 12th board exams she understood she had to clear the so called "Entrance Exams" to be able to take admission to a medical college. Her first attempt in JEE ended in a failure as she couldn't score well. Her dad was scared about her future and so he was scared to let her try once more.

She begged her father for one last chance and he agreed. She had to prove herself in midst of all relatives and family people doubting her journey.

Her hunt started with collection of books, study materials, finding the solutions with her teachers Partha sir who immensely taught her chemistry. Her favourite Arpita didi who taught her physics and her loving family of masimoni and Jhimli didi who played an important part for being a part of her journey. Last but not the least her Misti didi who taught her the most crucial part of the exam, who taught her biology like no one ever taught her. She poured her knowledge and gave her everything to make it work. She didn't look at time she just taught everything she could in her limited span of time.

It was a tiring doubtful journey as everyone else thought where there was no guarantee for the amount of work you do. But Geet couldn't look back and she had to give her best as she has already taken the risk of losing a year.

All said and done exams finally came and it was that time of the year when she had to do her best and secure a place for herself.

Chapter Two

The Ordeal

"The Ordeal" as she likes to quote was her ordeal with exams. It was like an entrance gate which she had to cross to be able to enter the greater world. As her father spent most of his time abroad due to his work he couldn't be physically present but always gave his support in her dreams. Few days before her exams her sister fell sick and she had to be rushed to a bigger city where she could avail the treatment. Her mother left with her sister. So now Geet was left alone with her domestic help in her house.

She continued her studies along with managing her house although she knew little so as to how to do that.

Exam day came finally and her uncle offered to drop her at her exam location. She refused but he was not ready to listen to it. He dropped her at her destined exam location.

Exam started. First paper… physics was a blow and she performed way below her expectations. The only thing she kept hope in was that she could manage to do well in her chemistry and biology papers.

Exams finished now it was time for results. She made it. She scored a place for herself. Now came the wait for the counselling process.

Chapter Three

The Journey

The journey as she quotes is the journey of her new life as an entrant to the medical college. She was absolutely clueless where she was going what college to choose where she would get a seat or whom to contact. She had no contacts no nearby whom she could enquire about anything related to this profession. She went ahead with whatever she felt right. Those days there was hardly much use of internet. She found an article in the newspaper about the counselling dates to be held in a government owned auditorium. She collected all documents required for the counselling process.

Finally, the day came. She was accompanied by her mother. The counselling process went on till evening and finally she was granted an MBBS seat in a government medical college in another state. She was happy but a certain dilemma prevailed in her mind about how it was all going to be.

Next big problem she gets allotted a seat on Saturday evening. She is being asked to report on Monday which meant she had to leave on Sunday which meant the next day morning itself.

Her mother didn't have an ATM card at that period of time and the only way for her to draw money was from the bank. Now Sunday is a holiday and there wasn't enough money in cash with them. Her dad was abroad and it was a helpless situation. Being a new place and little unsafe to travel alone due to certain political turmoil to her destined location, her uncle agreed to come along as he had travelled over there a couple of times. Being related to sports her uncle had a lot of juniors over there who have trained under him and they agreed to help them happily.

As there was no direct flight from her state to her destined college location she had to embark on a two way flight journey.

The next big problem was money. Although there was money in the account there was no provision to withdraw it because of Sunday being a holiday.

Much to her surprise her neighbour offered to help them and gave 50,000 in cash. Thank you was a very small word for his generosity. The flight agencies who booked their usual tickets offered to give the tickets at zero payment and assured them that they could travel then and make the payment later. So tickets for Geet, her mother and her uncle were booked. Another issue came up about documents which had to be duly attested by a Gazetted Officer by that day only. Now at that time at night where will they get a Gazetted Officer. Suddenly one name struck her mind her friend Aparajita's mother. She called her up and aunty asked her to come home. She went to her house at night 10 pm and happily aunty attested all her documents. She wished her all the best.

(Sadly aunty is no more but she will stay in memories for her kindness).

Geet came home running and now arose the question what to pack. She and her mother packed very few clothes for the next day journey. She woke up early next day checked all her documents and left home saying goodbye to everyone. She didn't have shops open to take new passport pictures for official purpose so she carried old ones with her. She started on her journey and took her first flight and there was a second connecting one too. As the distance was very less they were provided small flights accommodating about 20 to 30 people during her second flight. Finally, she reached and she could notice many more people accompanied by their parents and she guessed probably they might be her fellow batchmates. She didn't speak to them since she didn't know anyone. She collected her luggage. Her uncle's juniors came to pick them at the airport and they left together for the hotel.

✸ ✸ ✸

Chapter Four

First Impression

First impression as they always say is very true in certain circumstances. Her first impression after landing at the airport was a little confusing. She was not happy but a sense of doubt prevailed in her mind as to how everything was going to be. The airport was just ok very small but ok for a small place like that. As she stepped outside the airport a cab was booked and they left for the hotel. On her exit from the airport she noticed a beautiful Hindu temple which was very beautiful in midst of lush greenery. As the cab proceeded the city centre she was taken back at the condition of the capital city. The city looked like it was recovering post a war-torn phase. Very undermined structures, bad roads and what scared her the most was the rickshaw pullers with their face half covered. All she could see was their eyes. She was taken aback by the sight of the city and the general sight of people walking around. Geet always thought her hometown to be underdeveloped but for the first time she felt her hometown was like any other metro city and where she landed up was an outdated place. The shocking part was all the shops would close down by 4 pm as she was informed by the locals. Her cab made its way to a hotel which was very good compared to the outside scenario. Her uncle's juniors took tea with her mom and left. Mom asked them to have lunch but they promised to have it some other day and left. Uncle went to his room and took rest. Geet and mom finally went to bed after a long day's travel. The day ended with dinner and a good night sleep. In her mind Geet had hundreds of questions, hundreds of doubts how the next day would begin. Amidst all this turmoil, she managed to get some sleep and prepare for her big day.

Chapter Five

The Entrance

Geet woke up early in the morning and had a quick bath. She grabbed some breakfast and checked all her documents. To her mom's continuous request, she accepted to put on her mom's favourite yellow coloured frilled salwar. Geet always loved her short hair and she put some hair clips to fix her messy hair.

Mom, uncle and she left for the college. As they reached the college she realised the city was very dirty, clumsy and a difficult place to live in. The place was chaotic full of small open dirty markets smelling terrible. The first sight of the college was not at all appealing.

Now at the "Entrance" was the college gate which was broken about to perish in no time. The first conclusion Geet summarized in her mind was "badly managed institution". She still told herself probably it's a very old college that's why the gates are like that. The college name was not properly visible on the gate. She wondered in her mind if all Government run institutes were like that. She didn't know anything where was the entrance or where was the office. Uncle searched a little bit and found the

Principal's office as there were no proper instructions or signboards given anywhere.

Now comes the grand introduction ...... Geet finds a big batch of people standing at the entrance of the Principal's office. She first thinks they are her to be batchmates but quickly she understood they are her seniors waiting to introduce them to the so-called word "RAGGING". She also finds similar faces of people over there she saw at the airport and realised they were students who have also come for admission. She sensed a sudden nerve wrecking fear with all the people standing over there. All weird looking seniors, their horrible ways of staring at everyone...their unpleasant wicked smiles all brought turmoil in Geet's mind. They blocked the way to Principal's office and were not allowing anyone to go to the Principal's office. Geet wondered what college it was. Geet completed her entire schooling from a very disciplined school and her Principal was one of the best teachers anyone could ask for who taught them so much etiquettes and discipline in life that all that was happening before her eyes was difficult for her to digest or accept. She questioned herself as to how students had that much audacity to behave that way and how pathetic the college administration was to let the students do that.

Next step they pushed everyone's parents out of the entrance and asked them to wait outside. Geet's uncle and mom followed the instructions and waited outside. None of the students could meet the Principal or the Dean.

To her surprise all the admission forms were also with the seniors.

Now from her state, mixed race of students came for admission. Now the so called "Seniors" started segregating students based on their ethnicity and handed students of different ethnicity to their respective seniors.

As they discussed Geet could make out their plans and motives. All of her batchmates were taken in a classroom and given forms to fill up. She started filling up the form. Before she entered the classroom, her mother gave her the mobile phone. To much of her surprise her seniors noticed that very quickly. That time not everyone had a mobile phone. Geet's dad purchased that mobile phone long back and gave it to her mom so that she could speak to him whenever she wanted as he was working abroad. While she was filling up the form one of her senior came and told her what all to fill up as she was quietly sitting on the bench and filling up the form. Quickly she realised his attention was towards her blue coloured flipflop phone. He started asking her from where she purchased the phone to which she bluntly answered her dad got it. Next question actually was not really a question rather to be quoted as a command "Give me the phone". Geet stopped writing she lifted her head up and tried to understand what really he tried to mean. She realised very quickly that she didn't hear it wrong. She grabbed her hands and answered him boldly but politely that it's her mother's phone and she couldn't give it to him. Next what followed still gives her chills down her spine even after so many years. He came to slap her. Tears started rolling down her eyes and she was frozen in that moment not able to accept what was happening over there. He stopped his hands. Senior's speech "Please save your tears and collect them as there is water shortage in the hostel". That very moment she summarised in short her future journey in the college. An immense sense of insecurity prevailed in her mind and she started getting scared at every sight of a senior. She submitted the form and gave all photocopies of all her documents. This very step saved her life she realised it later.

Chapter Six

Rules

Geet knew from the beginning that medical profession required a lot of discipline. But she never knew about those rules her seniors had self written or better to frame it as a protocol for the juniors. To her astonishment she came to know that all her other batchmates knew about all that and were well informed.

Geet heard a lot about ragging history from her mother how her neighbours few of them who attempted to study couldn't take this journey as a medico and called it quits. She understood probably her batchmates have known previous pass outs from this college who have kept them well informed.

There was nothing called rules it was their dirty minds and their dirty ways to have fun with people so that the juniors suffer and they can enjoy seeing them suffer.

Next day as advised by the great "Seniors" Geet went to the college as she was told the formalities were not yet over. Little did she know that formalities meant a way of bringing students together to spend more time on ragging.

Fresh question of the day "Where are you staying?".

Geet politely answered Hotel Kristina and what follows is the same ritual what happened the day before an attempt to slap. Geet closed her eyes and tears rolled down her eyes again. She tried to control her tears. For a moment she couldn't hear anything. All her vision was blurred. She had never encountered anyone speaking so loudly to her. She was trying to get hold of the entire situation.

Her seniors started asking her if she was a princess that she had to stay in that hotel. He just yelled at her and said "By today afternoon pack your bags and come to Dharamsala".

Now what is Dharamsala? As much divine the name sounds that much dirty that place was.

To her surprise she found out except her all others were staying over there from the first day.

All her batchmates landed directly to the so called Dharamsala. She didn't know how all these happened. She wondered if they had contacted the seniors before or they knew that it was a usual ritual.

She didn't speak much to anyone since she didn't know anyone but among all she found two of her batchmates to be different from all of them. Soumyadeep and Joydeep… she connected with them very well and found her comfort zone with them. She bonded with their families also very well.

She asked them about Dharamsala because she felt she could rely on them. All she heard from them is that "Pack your bags and come soon to Dharamsala". Geet was all panicky and could not understand anything but she was scared as hell.

Joydeep's uncle and parents had accompanied him. Soumyadeep was accompanied by his parents. Their families became her family. They cared for her as much they cared for their own kin.

She spoke about it to her mom and uncle. They initially hesitated but later realised things should not be difficult for Geet as she had to stay there with her seniors.

Geet always heard it from others that this ragging will be just an initial phase and later all your seniors will become your friends. She understood it very quick that it was all nonsense and this ragging process never ended.

She like all others felt she didn't have options and agreed to shift to Dharamsala.

So she went back to hotel. Geet's mom cleared all the bills. Uncle also packed the bags and they all left for Dharamsala the next day. Before they left the hotel the night before they had dinner as promised before with uncle's juniors.

Chapter Seven

Dharamsala

Dharamsala: The name sounds so divine. After you finish reading this chapter you will hate this name like nothing you have ever hated before. Even the slight sound of the word "Dharamsala" terrified Geet like nothing else.

As local transport system was terrible the only quick option for them was to hire a car. Geet and her family put their bags and set on their journey to Dharamsala.

The distance was not much between their hotel and that place.

First sight of the place … Geet couldn't step in so easily. She never saw such a terrible looking hotel in her entire life. Being a well-travelled girl, she has stayed in every sort of hotel but she never saw anything of this sort.

Uncle and mom too were at shock to see the place. Now everyone must be thinking what is this place that Geet was so terrified of.

"Dharamsala" was a non local community run lodge which was filthy beyond your imagination which was cheap as hell and very quickly Geet and her family realised that above all there was no safety or security in that lodge. Anyone was free to come in and go. It was like a grass field where all cattle are free to roam.

Uncle went and booked two rooms. Unfortunately, they couldn't find two rooms together. So Geet and mom took one room which was facing the balcony near the market place. Uncle got one room near the first floor entrance.

Quickly Geet could locate her batchmates with their families all in the same floor. Only Joydeep was located in the 4th floor. It was a huge lodge probably four or five storeyed. All the rooms had one basic dhaba style iron cot. One light with one fan, single window with rods placed outside and a fragile door which had no sense of security. Only the hotel people knew how long they haven't cleaned it or repaired the furniture. There was no lift so they had to drag all the luggage till the first floor. Thank God her room was in the first floor as there was no help available to help them with the luggage.

The people at the reception were terrible all sold at the hands of money.

Now you must be thinking how can she comment like that … read till the end and you will hate them even more than Geet did.

All the floors had only one bathroom which had no light only one tap and one toilet. So they went to the nearby market and bought buckets and mugs so that they could take bath. Uncle came to know that most of the time by evening power supply goes off and it doesn't come for hours so they bought candles and matchboxes also. They didn't have a generator in the lodge. They didn't realise all these till the time they were in the first hotel. The next terrible thing they found out is that everything shuts down by 4 pm so they have to get food, water bottles and all necessary stuff before that. There was no provision to get drinking water in the lodge. Sometimes there would be no water in the washroom so everyone should store water for that. There was nothing called hot water available over there.

Every floor had 15 to 16 rooms and one bathroom, one washroom which was the lifeline for everyone. There used to be one asbestos sheet door which used to be the door for the bathroom. To be able to take bath one had to get to the bathroom by 5/5:30 am because after that there is a huge queue for bathroom. The bathroom door had no proper lock only a wire which you have to wind round to keep the door closed. So you have to be real quick to finish all your bathing and so on.

Now comes the most terrible part of this dirty place so called as "Dharamsala". This was less of a lodging place and more of a ragging place. All the staff of this lodge were paid money by the seniors in Geet's college to officially allow them to come and rag them inside the lodge.

Everyday evening after classes all the dirty "seniors" used to come over there drag all the students to the rooftop … do all the terrible things they wanted to and leave for their heavenly hostel by night 9 or sometimes even late than this.

The rooms didn't even have blankets so they started using bedsheets as blankets which Geet thought she would use in the hostel.

Now the juniors were being told that hostel rooms were not available and till then they would have to stay in Dharamsala. Now that was a big fat lie everything including allotment of hostel was controlled by the seniors which she understood later. Geet thought what was really happening did she come to study or bear atrocities of her seniors. But like everyone she didn't have options. She must have thought it would end over there but what lies ahead she didn't imagine in her dreams also.

She understood one thing this hostel allotment was being handled by the seniors and although hostels were available they purposefully delayed it.

She started picturing the next days and was quickly losing her peace of mind. She still silently waited for the worst that was about to happen.

* * *

Chapter Eight

Introduction To Ragging

Ragging a very popular word in colleges what in Western world they call it bullying. It is a word every college student is familiar with. Geet always heard from her mother that medical colleges have terrible ragging and you should overcome that part in order to finish your studies. It was like a testing phase every medical entrant had to go through for some it was just basic introduction and for some it was beyond description.

The day she shifted to Dharamsala was her first day of the grand introduction with ragging.

She went to college and she was told by evening seniors would come to visit them. At first, she thought maybe they wanted to know them better, speak to them, or guide them regarding the next phase of their new life as a medico.

Now Geet and all her batchmates came back to Dharamsala after college. She thought in her mind she would come back, freshen up and take some rest. All hell came together. Before they reached Dharmasala all their seniors were waiting for them.

The way they looked at them seemed like all juniors were their prey like a vulture preys on its food. Nothing was welcoming over there. All the lodge reception people were talking, sharing jokes with the seniors. It was as if everything was a staged drama they were just characters to be played about. All juniors were walking past the seniors as if they were walking past some dictator who has officially captured that area.

All juniors wished the seniors. "Come fast to the rooftop" maggot seniors shouted. Geet and her batchmates ran to their rooms to keep their bags. This time Geet saw a new bunch of people in addition to the old useless bunch which included girls among which she noticed one short, little overweight girl looking at her as if she has found the perfect candidate. She realised very soon that this very lady was none other than Suparna whom Geet's mom very lovingly quoted her as "Surpanakha" because she had all the evil nature of that character. All of them rushed fast to the rooftop which meant 5th floor.

5th floor had few rooms also. So Geet like all her other batchmates rushed to their rooms. No time for lunch they all rushed to 5th floor. Geet's uncle and mom also accompanied her like all others were accompanied by their parents. They all went to 5th floor and went to one empty room on the 5th floor which was facing the rooftop.

Geet and all others noticed one thing which was not at all appealing a huge group of people were standing at the rooftop which was bigger than what they saw at the entrance. All of them figured out that the bigger problem was already waiting at the rooftop. All of them were staring as if they were waiting for the perfect prey. Geet felt a quench in her heart but she was helpless like others. Slowly they all walked out of the room towards the rooftop. All parents waited inside the room feeling helpless not knowing what was going to happen.

Geet and all other batchmates walked towards the seniors. None of the seniors were smiling. Rude as hell they can be all of them started calling each one of the students as per their choices. It was like everyone got their perfect prey. It was as if all the parents were seated in an auditorium to watch a live show of what was going to happen with their kin.

First question "How many of you have studied from regional medium and how many from English medium?". Geet noticed there was one silent very gentle guy in her batch whom she came to know later that his name was Akash was the one of the few kids amongst the group of 13 to 14 people who belonged to English medium apart from Geet. One more guy was also from English medium school with whom Geet hardly spoke. So being from different education mediums they were meant to have different treatment ... not really in the right sense.

Her first interaction was with a senior probably in 3rd year of MBBS. First introduction "What is your name? Where are you from? What was your rank?". She answered everything politely. Next question was to assess her financial status which of course first started with "What is your parent's occupation? What is their education? Where do they work?". Once Geet answered all these questions all the faces changed. Guess what Geet said …… "My Dad works abroad". Some started smiling at her and some saw her as the perfect prey. Some other seniors took her and started asking her what was the name of the bone around the neck. Geet didn't know that time that particular bone was called "clavicle". She answered "It is called collar bone" as she heard this bone being called collar bone by her mom and uncles since her childhood. Geet thought the questions would end there but the next question really shook her. "Where is your collar bone?". Geet was a little surprised what sort of a question was that. She didn't say anything. The nonsense answer her senior gave was … "You are fat that's why your collar bone can't be seen as it is embedded in your fat". Geet was not hurt but for a moment she thought does anyone really comment on how they look so terribly and what did they think of themselves as if they were some dudes. Tears did come to her eyes but she controlled them.

Now comes the grand introduction to the bosses and ladies of this useless waste bunch of seniors. Very quickly she realised the audacity of the people over there didn't depend on the seniority but on your quality how much terrible you can be. "The worse the merrier". She like all others kept on shifting her place since 4 or 5 pm till night 9/9:30 pm. All her batchmates were tired but they were not spared. Like her they were also standing all day long. In the college they won't allow them to attend classes they would make them stand for ragging. Back in the lodge also they would stand.

Geet quickly noticed two of her school seniors Anupam and Anirban. She felt a ray of hope but she never dreamt in her deadliest dreams that they would be the worst of the lot. She had a brief introduction with them. She addressed them as elder brother but in a spat of minute they yelled back at her "ONLY SIR". Geet said sorry and addressed them as Sir.

The next in their line was what are the poems they all knew. Everyone kept wondering who remembers those childhood poems. Suddenly Anupam came and asked Geet to narrate Baba black sheep, Jack and Jill. All in a minute she started telling the poems all in a flow as if she was back to her old nursery days. What followed next shocked her.

They demanded the recent revised version of Jack and Jill. Geet was all confused what the hell were they asking. It was not some physics law which has been modified so what it could be. Please read the next paragraph carefully…

Jack and Jill went up the hill

To fetch a pail of water

Jack went up Jill went up

Came back with a baby together.

Then comes the next question to Geet "How did the baby come with them?". Geet was frozen for a moment. She didn't understand the question for a moment later she didn't know what she was hearing, what to say, what to answer. She kept quiet. They started yelling at her to tell the process.

Next turn from another dirty senior "Narrate Newton's Third law". Geet answered all like forces attract each other unlike forces repel each other. For her surprise they narrated a perverted version of Newton's law. Geet cursed in her mind how dare they make perverted versions of such a great scientist's hard work. They should rot in hell.

This series of their perverted knowledge continued. They wrote all of them in a piece of paper and gave copies to all of them. They asked all of them to share the copies and learn it by heart. They also informed that the next day they will have to tell it fluently to all seniors. Geet handed her paper to another batchmate and she didn't open the paper as she promised in her mind she would never read such dirty poems. As much calm and quiet Geet was, she was always a rebel at heart.

So much horrible things she heard that entire evening that she found it hard to believe if they really were medical students. Everyone had terrible sessions of harassment, bullying, hearing things no one ever thought existed in a medical college. All of them were post 12th standard just few days outside their homes and everything was so terrible that it was hard to accept. Geet still thought in her mind all medical pass out experiences says the same thing this is just few days and in the end you all are going to be friends.

The seniors left past 9 pm. All parents were sitting in the room watching all that happened over there. Everyone understood their kids are going to have a tough time.

Since there was no provision of getting dinner at night Geet and her family had something whatever foodstuff they had and slept off. Geet was tired like hell but she couldn't fall asleep. A sense of fear prevailed and she wondered what was left for the next days. Finally she slept holding her mother.

Chapter Nine

Introduction to Seniors

All beloved seniors ... let them be introduced. Without them being introduced the entire book will be incomplete. All of them belonged to the same state as she belonged to. They had one rule only people from same state will be handed to same state seniors. Also, even if they are from the same state they will be ragged only by the people from same ethnic group. That was a treaty among all these people.

First person Geet encountered in the college was Prasun ... the extra tall guy who was so thin with a mole on the face with a wicked smile on his face ... he acted like the father figure for all basically he was searching for a perfect girl he could prey on. His signature style was his Rudraksh necklace which he wore all the time. On one occasion during the ragging sessions he removed his Rudraksh necklace and asked Geet to put it on any of the guy's she liked over there. She refused to do so and she faced terrible consequences.

Next on the list was Sourav … one dusky complexioned short heighted overweight guy whose house was not very far from Geet's house in her hometown. He tried to develop a romantic relationship with Geet but he never succeded. Even people started calling Geet as Dona.

Next on the list comes two of her beloved seniors from school Anupam and Anirban both were probably in their third year of medical school. Before she left for her medical school, her school history teacher mentioned Anupam's name as Geet was not aware of him studying in the same college. She like her teachers felt he might be of help as both were from the same school. He turned out to be the worst among all. He was from an English medium school so his attitude was a little more than his fellow batchmates who were from a regional medium. He was a prominent figure amongst all probably because of his looks. Geet earlier heard about Anupam's elder brother during her school days who was equally terrible like him and showed hell to juniors in his engineering college. Anupam's language was dirty like garbage. He would speak all rubbish language with everyone more with girls but at the end all he would say "Sorry. I am taken". Geet knew the girl with whom he had a relationship very well as she was also from her school.

Next in the list of prominent people was Anirban who was also from her school. He was equally terrible but a little less than Anupam. He was basically Anupam's apprentice.

Monirul, the nasty guy from the interiors of her state, was a huge guy with the nastiest mind. He couldn't be compared to anything on this earth so much dirt is filled inside him.

One good guy she found in the entire lot was Gourishankar who was in his final year who was only senior by name but had no power. He was a mere puppet at the hands of his juniors. He used to come along with them but never harassed anyone. He tried saving people wherever possible. Later Geet came to know even he used to get bashing from his team people as he was not like them. He was the single decent guy in the entire lot.

The worst of the lot … Shyamrup … fair complexioned medium heighted guy with a frameless specs … he was like a vulture scanning everything that was going around him. He knew how to preside over everything and give his dirty valuable suggestions to make things worse and he always had ideas how to make juniors suffer more. He used to be omnipresent but his ideas used to work through everyone else's minds. Though he was a final year student there was no signs of being so. Geet always wondered she heard final year students don't have time to breathe from where did he get time to get involved in this nonsense ragging.

Like these the list is never ending. She didn't even want to recollect at one point of time.

Few names she couldn't forget in the list. This might look like so much negativity to some but these names are must in this list.

There were very few ladies among the seniors. Although they were less, all of them were pathetic and horrible in every aspect. Geet always thought girls would be more considerate towards other girls but to her surprise they turned to be more horrible than the guys. Words would fall short to describe them.

Suparna, a short heighted, not-so-thin, wheatish complexioned girl, was the probable leader of the entire group. She was terrible in every way you could think of. She noticed Geet from the first day and made her the prime target. Not only Geet all her batchmates … everyone had their share of sufferings but above all she faced the maximum. She troubled Geet so much and she misbehaved with her mom so much she was coined by the name "Surpanakha" by her mother as she had all the evil qualities of that character. She had no respect for any parents and spoke to them in singulars. Her favourite dialogue was "We have turned back one student from this college. We compelled him to leave the course now what he will do … he might work just as a mere postman. But as soon as I passout I will draw a minimum salary of 65k". Geet wondered what a terrible lady she was who was proud of the fact that she ragged some state topper who had come to study here securing good rank in the entrance exams. She tortured him so much along with her batchmates that he had to leave this course. In her mind Geet cursed this lady for spoiling someone's future and singing about it as an achievement. She used to repeat the same thing and terrorise people.

She had an accomplice Sampa who was so fragile and tall that she might break down at any point … but she was equally shrill in her nonsense activities.

And the list went on ……

Chapter Ten

Fellows and Families

Fellows were none other than her batchmates. Though 19 students were there in her batch of 100 people from her state but soon on the first day they were segregated by seniors according to their ethnicity.

She figured out they were group of 12 to 13 students after separation was done.

Although there were so many of them she got along only with few of them.

She had only two friends in true sense.

Soumyadeep and Joydeep … their families all of them were angels in disguise.

Both of them belonged to her city but she didn't know anyone of them till she joined this medical college.

Soumyadeep was the first person she saw at the airport but she didn't speak as she didn't know him but guessed he was one of her probable batchmates.

Joydeep's family connected to her first later she became friends with him. Joydeep's family had one connection with Geet's uncle as Joydeep's uncle who had accompanied them was also from the sports background and was also a teacher like Geet's uncle. They bonded very well. Gradually his mom became very close to Geet. They always cared for Geet as much they cared for their own son whether it was her safety, food or health. Words would fall short for whatever they did for her. Whenever they used to bring some food for their son they used to share it with her. They became her family. She has never met such a kind family like them.

How can Geet forget Soumyadeep or Somu as called by everyone … specially his parents. She was always grateful for their care. His mom used to ask about Geet everyday if she didn't get to see her in the college.

Their families saved her life and no words would describe what she felt for their selfless care for her.

Another silent character was Akash who was accompanied by his mom Geeta aunty who was not only extremely beautiful on the outside but she had a beautiful heart too. She was extremely quiet, soft spoken and humble. In one word if anyone had to quote Akash it would be a good boy. Geet felt terrible whenever she heard those dirty senior boys discussing about Geeta aunty's beauty. She wondered if they were even human or they have lost all morals. She would always greet Geet with a smile.

She found one familiar face amongst all the guys who used to study biology with her in the same tuition. Since his mom was not well he was only accompanied by his dad. Geet had lot of sympathy for him since his mom was having terminal illness but to her shock he also turned out to be terrible. She avoided speaking to him as she figured out what he was doing very early.

The other guys in her batch were only hi bye for her she really never spoke to them.

There were very few girls hardly 4 or 5 among the entire lot. Geet never bonded with a single lady. It's not because she didn't try to bond but very quickly she understood one thing she should refrain from one thing which they were quite a pro was gossiping.

The most prominent character amongst them was Sangeeta who was a very beautiful intelligent female but looks can be deceiving as they say was very true in her case. She would sit quietly and observe everything. As much good she was in her studies that much she was good in catching attention. Soon she became the spot light and all seniors were talking about her. There was a competition who could impress and date her. Geet already knew that few seniors were making rounds of her and were in regular talks with her as they have exchanged numbers. Geet was least bothered as all she wanted was peace of mind and safety.

Another female who was very popular for the wrong reasons was Nivedita ... a fragile lady who might fly off if wind blew. She had nice voluminous hair with reddish to burgundy coloured streaks which disappeared within the 2nd or 3rd day of college. Seniors yelled at her and she had to colour her hair black. She became a target for Anupam because of her bold nature and non-hesitant reply. She used to answer to every question asked to her unlike Geet who preferred not answering for most of the questions. Her dressing also caught attention of all seniors. Her mom accompanied her to the college every day.

There were two more ladies with whom Geet avoided conversations as they enjoyed spreading words from senior to senior and causing trouble for others.

Very soon Geet realised that except Joydeep, Somu and Akash and their families, all other families accepted a policy of sidelining Geet and others they didn't like. They started conversations with seniors and they were doing all these thinking these would save their kids from all the sufferings that was following and would continue. They started exchanging gossips and seniors started targeting juniors about whom they heard all the gossips as created by the parents and Geet became the prime target. Things became worse day by day. Geet didn't understand how could parents do that along with students. "Where did their morals go then?".

Very quickly Geet figured out she had just two friends whom she could rely on ... Soumyadeep and Joydeep ... but she was not sad with the fact how others turned out to be. Akash being the silent good guy always stayed to his terms and didn't entertain any nonsense though he also was not spared.

Soumyadeep and Joydeep's families became her family. They cared for her as their own child and she felt grateful for that every second.

Chapter Eleven

Extremes (Five Days)

Extremes meant the extremes of ragging. As it might seem to some people what is there to brag so much about ragging Geet felt only the person who went through the horrific experience would understand that. She always had one question in her mind who were these people? They were students like her probably one or two years senior to her. Who gave them the right to beat juniors harass them speak garbage like language to them? Did their parents send them to study or do all these? Now some moral policing people would comment this is age old tradition …traditions are to be continued which are healthy, enriches a civilization rather than which demolishes human values.

What were the college management doing when they knew everything? "Did they also enjoy students being tortured like that?". Each student worked day and night to get a medical seat and is this what they get in return. They came to study a new branch not to get scared for their own life.

The ragging process was terrible as it started from morning college hours every day and it followed till Dharamsala. Every day was like an ordeal as if Geet waited the day to end soon and she wished the next day should never start. Her sleep was all gone. She started realising every move of hers was being followed. Even if she went out of Dharamsala there were people who were watching her from the hotel. As there was lot of political turmoil in that area, she and her mom had to get food and water for them before 4 pm as everything was shut down after that. All they could see after 4 pm was abandoned streets with all Army patrolling the areas. She once saw about 100 to 150 people being made to suddenly sit in knee bent position near to the main road just in front of Dharamsala. All army dressed people were checking their IDs. Everything was so scary over there. She even heard stories where a lady was killed in the hotel while she was standing at the balcony of the hotel when a bomb blast happened. She thought if all her other batchmates also felt like her or she was the only one feeling odd one out. She was losing interest in everything in life, medicine no more mattered to her and she like all her other batchmates were hardly allowed to attend classes to which she kept wondering if this continued how she would appear for exams as definitely there would be attendance shortage. Moreover, she would be out of track. She would not be able to study as she felt due to all the missed classes and medicine being a completely different branch from everything she had studied till now. Nothing seemed good to her but she like all others just said to herself "Hold on for a minute".

She thought slowly it would reduce but this was just introduction the real trailer was yet to come. All hell broke on 5th day after she landed in that horrible place.

As always, all the nonsense seniors came to Dharamsala. That day their happiness doubled and they were smiling like a cunning fox to which Geet had a lot of bad feeling. Even their voices scared her.

Their level was double than the previous days but what they spoke next made Geet dizzy. She found it difficult to accept that.

"From today you all are like birds in a cage … 5 days are over and your time to surrender this seat is over and now you can't apply for second round of counselling"

One thing became clear to everyone over there including Geet that now the real torture is about to start.

Geet had hundreds of questions in her mind going on at that moment what worse could happen. She never thought in her wildest dreams that now things would all turn to physical torture.

"Surpanakha" came towards Geet and the first thing she spoke was "You are so good we can't let you be so clean". This very statement didn't make any sense to Geet. All she knew was that how much dirty a person that lady was, there was definitely some big trouble coming in Geet's way. Suparna aka "Surpanakha" asked Geet to repeat some dirty phrases and words either having some sexual content or some degraded language that too in her pathetic low lying words with a dirty accent. Geet and all her seniors used to speak the same language as they all belonged to the same state but their way of speaking and accent was way far different. Geet had never heard of such language in her life as she never heard her parents speak like that. Geet was brought up by a very strict disciplined mom and her father who taught her a lot of etiquettes and manners. Whatever was happening around her was difficult for her to even dream in the rarest of her dreams. Being raised up in different regions of their origin state, everybody including her seniors and batchmates had different accent and words of the same language which became a hurdle for Geet to understand. She found it very difficult to understand what was being spoken to her. Only people who spoke to her the way she spoke were Somu, Joydeep and Akash.

When they wanted Geet to speak their way to which she could not, the level of their abuse increased. Till that day she only bore verbal abuse of her seniors but that day she started receiving physical abuse. Suparna and her aide Sampa both started yelling at Geet as Geet refused to speak their way and they started pulling her hair. They spoke horrible things to which Geet could not revolt because she understood that they were nothing but dictators and that place belonged to them.

Later at night when all hell finished at about 10 pm starting from 5 pm after all those 5 hours of standing and bearing all the torture, she ran to her room in tears. Her mom was also terrified at her daughter's sight. She quickly opened her file containing all her documents and took out her nomination letter from the state Government. She held out the letter and it was clearly written in that within 5 days she should surrender the seat to be eligible for a second round of counselling. Tears rolled down her cheek because one thing was clear to her now that she is trapped, she had only one option to bear all these or leave the seat. She looked at her mom because she could not even think of leaving the seat as it was her only option left now. Her mom was scared and crying too understanding what that letter meant and what was in store for her daughter. She wondered if she was the only one who didn't know this rule or she was the only one who didn't read it properly out of happiness of securing a medical seat. She sat and cried the entire night till she fell asleep.

Chapter Twelve

Uncle's Departure

Geet's uncle accompanied her and he promised to finish the admission process. He planned to return back after the admission to his hometown that is Geet's house as they all lived together in the same house as he had to get back to his job. Geet's uncle visited many medical colleges before as he went with many of his colleague's kids during their admission. He was very surprised at the behaviour of students over there. He accompanied Geet along with her mom to her college as they both were scared like hell that something wrong would happen to her on her way back to Dharamsala. They both knew they were not going to be there over there forever but still they went with Geet just to pacify their minds. Geet didn't know the local language and that scared them more. Uncle being in the sports background had a lot of known to people from the football fraternity and he found out one of the person running one of the canteens in the campus was his old colleague in football clubs.

As Geet stepped out of the class her mom and uncle took her to the canteen. First, she didn't eat anything;

secondly, uncle wanted to introduce her to his friend as he thought a local known to would be of great help. The canteen uncle was very well aware of the terrible things that went on in that college and all he could say was come to my house if you feel bad or call me anytime. She tried a few things in his canteen which was better than other places she tried in the city. There was hardly any good food in the city. Geet was staying in the city proper and every food she tried was terrible. She often thought if the capital city was like that than what would be the condition of outskirts. She didn't like the local food too. She knew deep down in her mind that even if she knew that canteen uncle, nothing was going to change.

That day in the evening when that nonsense gang came to the rooftop of Dharamsala, Geet's mom and uncle went to the rooftop and sat in an empty room along with other guardians. They were petrified of the situation and felt helpless. Geet's uncle literally wanted to go and grab their collars and ask them "Don't you people have anything to study?". She always heard during her schooling that medicos don't have time to breathe than what all these nonsense people were doing. Slowly she came to know that there is a long list of people who didn't clear their MBBS degree till then some for almost 10 years in the college. She understood if they continued doing these than when would they study so it was quite natural for them to drag on for years and on.

As 5 days passed their violence increased. Geet understood one thing every batchmate of hers had a certain group of seniors. Seniors self appointed themselves as mentors. No one was allowed to move from their place where they were standing till they told them to do so. Geet looked around and saw all the batchmates having a tough time verbally and physically abused. She heard Anupam saying to one of the girls "I will rape you just come to the hostel". She just thought if she could run away from there.

She figured out the boys were beaten up like hell and maximum inflict was on Somu and Joydeep. Her heart broke seeing everybody suffering so much that she could not hold her tears. Geet's family like all others could not bear the sight and walked down.

One dirty senior came and asked Geet what was her uncle doing there. She didn't speak a word because she didn't want to answer their dirty questions. In response to her silence he started telling if she came there to study medicine or she wanted to become a footballer like her uncle. She couldn't bear disrespect towards her uncle but she kept quiet with her head down tears rolling down her cheek.

Sourav tried to be her saviour and started taking her away from others and he spoke very gently to her compared to others. Very soon she realised he was just gathering information about her family and assessing her status. She also quickly realised he used to be drunk most of the times but very much well tolerated. She started avoiding him and this caught attention of everyone including her batchmates. Akash started calling her as "Dona" after the name of famous Indian cricketer Sourav Ganguly's wife's name.

Uncle had to get back to his work and her admission process was over except the fact that she and her batchmates didn't get a hostel appointed. She quickly realised hostel allotment was also done by these people and that is the reason it is being delayed.

Geet's uncle and Joydeep's uncle both left. Mom got his ticket done through their agency. Uncle told his juniors Khamba uncle and Chanu aunty to take care of them. He also requested them to look after Geet even when her mom eventually had to leave for home.

Uncle left for airport but the flight was cancelled. Since both uncle and Joydeep's uncle were going by the same flight they decided to stay back at the same hotel provided by the Airlines as a compensation. Uncle called and informed Geet's mom the same and Geet's mom too nodded to his decision as the hotel was nearer to the airport. Next day he left but he kept in touch with them.

✳ ✳ ✳

Chapter Thirteen

Violence

At the airport the previous day uncle met Shyamrup. He was travelling by the same flight. He recognised uncle and uncle started a conversation with him. Initially they were not informed of the cancellation of the flight so like all other passengers uncle found him sitting at the waiting room waiting to board the flight.

His attention caught at Shyamrup sitting next to him. Uncle spoke to him and he too started speaking to uncle. Uncle casually asked him if he was going home to which he nodded yes. He also asked uncle the same and uncle replied yes as his leaves were over and he had to get back to work. Uncle casually asked him why did they all do this torture to all juniors they were all like his brother and sister. What he replied was out of this world … "Can't you see we are making your kids smart?". Uncle lost words as he understood what degree degraded person he was. Uncle didn't speak a word after that. As the flight was cancelled and scheduled for the next day, uncle along with Joydeep's uncle moved to the provided hotel as provided by the airline's office. Uncle reached the hotel and called Geet's mom that this all happened. They spoke over the phone.

Geet went for her prescheduled ragging sessions at the rooftop. Geet saw Shyamrup sitting over there. Geet had no idea if he was going home and that he met uncle at the airport since she was stuck up with those nasty people over the rooftop. There was a flat cement slab on the rooftop near the water tank on which all the so called dignified men were sitting and waiting for that day's drama to unfold.

All these men made Geet stand in front of her. Shyamrup started to talk to the rest of them and eventually she got to know that he was supposed to go home but his flight was cancelled. What next followed was all lies. Shyamrup said "Geet's uncle was misbehaving and scolding me at the airport about all this ragging stuff. I didn't say anything".

Geet's heart thumped. She knew troubles became doubled. All present over there started yelling at her and telling her what does she think of herself. They started asking her if she really wanted to continue her studies over there. She was shocked as they were literally threatening her over which she had no clues. She realised they were like pests of that place. They didn't come to study but to spoil people's lives. She was mumb over what really happened and what she really did to which they were behaving like that. She knew one thing for sure her uncle did nothing wrong and it was all cooked up by Shyamrup.

Following this they were hurling her with verbal abuses and the same statement kept flowing that she better behaves properly so that she can stay over there. She couldn't recollect what happened that all these stuffs were happening.

Shyamrup started the order of tasks as they quote it as ragging. He asked her to make all the sounds that happens while passing stools. By the way from the first day they asked her to stand with head bowed down all the time till they left the lodge. The immense amount of neck pain she and others faced was beyond words. Geet standing there with her head bowed down as advised by them from the first day which they try to make it look dignified as "Anatomical position", had tears rolling down her eyes. Now what is this "Anatomical position"?

Anatomical position as refined by them was standing straight with head bowed down, hands straight and palms facing upwards. Certain days they had to stand like that for 4 to 5 hours. At the end of the day along with tears she used to carry terrible back and neck pain. She realised she was falling sick because of all these atrocities.

Geet stood there crying to which all of them started yelling at her. She didn't have options other than creating certain sounds. She started crying more but they didn't stop. They started asking her to show the different postures of passing stools. She just felt if she had any chances of running from that place she would run from that place leaving everything. She just showed them squatting posture to which they were rolling over there in laughter. Still they didn't stop the next task was to make sounds of stools passing during diarrhoea and also to include in between farting sounds. Geet couldn't control her tears. They were yelling at her like never before but she couldn't stop crying. She stood still over there and didn't speak a word. She was then dragged by Surpanakha. She asked her to roll on the ground. Geet started rolling on the ground following which she was asked to swim. As she didn't have any options she pretended to swim lying on the floor. Whenever she stopped rolling Surpanakha started hitting her on the nape of her neck with her umbrella which she was carrying that day probably the day being a little cloudy. Suparna had a bottle of water which she was sprinkling on her as she was rolling. After sometime it stopped. What followed next was terrible. They asked her to say something in their slang which she said she couldn't as she never spoke in that slang. Surpanakha and Sampa both of them carried a bottle of mustard oil which they started pouring on Geet's head. Mustard oil started drooling from her hair to her eyes. Her eyes started burning and her cry was inconsolable now. All the nasty people over there were laughing out so loud as if it was the biggest joke on earth.

She looked around and saw Somu and Joydeep being made to stand on one leg. As many times they lost their balance they were being beaten up. She sobbed as she never saw anything more terrible than this. Most of the guys were being beaten up so badly for once she thought what dreams all of them came there with and what hell it turned out to be. Next whatever they were yelling at her she became numb she couldn't hear anything. Nothing was penetrating her ears. All she did was cry louder bowing her head down. She was feeling so helpless. On the contrary she saw the other girls were less tortured. They were standing at certain spots with their designated seniors and they were singing or dancing but no beating sessions. Geet had no idea what was going on but she could not wrap up her head to anything that was happening. They made her propose to 16 seniors bending on one knee and at the end of each session all she heard was "You, fat girl, who will even look at you". They were such nasty pests she felt wherever they would go they would just spread sadness. They made her dance initially and then sing continuously.

Simultaneously they made Soumyadeep dance. If she finished her song and didn't start another they used to beat him. At last after so long she couldn't recollect songs, so Somu requested her to repeat the same songs and he would keep dancing or else he would get beaten up.

They were exhausted no food, no water and on top of that this torture.

It became very dark and the only light was from the bulbs hanging at the corridor. Prasun, Anupam, Suparna and few more took Geet to the extreme end of the rooftop where the walls were ending. It was the extreme end where the building ended. The wall was not very high and one could put their leg outside easily. They asked Geet to put one leg outside the wall. Geet stood there shocked to what she was hearing. They screamed at the top of their voices. She didn't have any option other than putting one leg outside the wall. Everything was dark and all she could see was pitch black darkness below the wall. She wondered if she fell down what would be down … pointed iron bars or something else. Those nasty people didn't stop there. Now they wanted her to put the other leg too. She thought that was her end and she could imagine the next step. They might push her or she herself would fall after losing balance and they would frame it as suicide. She closed her eyes and as she was about to put the other leg she heard a voice saying "STOP". She saw Gaurishankar running towards them. He asked her to immediately come inside the rooftop. He helped her. He screamed at them and said "Have you all gone mad?". Geet still dizzy from what just happened could not stand still. Gaurishankar started speaking to them in a loud voice as if they even bothered to realise what would have happened if she fell down. He told

Geet to go down and subsequently all her batchmates went down. They finally thought it was called a day. Gaurishankar called Geet and all her batchmates in one room and asked them to wait. Geet just wanted to run away and hug her mother.

She sat on the cot along with her other female batchmates and the guys stood in the room. Geet kept on crying. Gaurishankar told everyone whatever was happening was very bad and whatever they all were doing to Geet was unacceptable. Geet suddenly looked up astonished as she didn't understand anything what he was talking. He even mentioned "You people should stop saying bad things about each other to seniors and rather stay by each other's side". Now everything was crystal clear to her it's her female batchmates and their parents who were spreading the poison about her to seniors by speaking ill about her. That was their trick to save their kids. They were all from regional medium schools and never liked Geet being from an English medium school. Geet never understood what was in their minds and for what they did that to her as she hardly spoke to them unless they spoke.

Geet ran to her room hugged her mom and cried like she never cried before. She told her mom everything.

Mom called uncle and told him everything. Uncle reached home by then and was shocked to hear how much lies Shyamrup told everyone and made her suffer. In front of her room there was a market where she could see a hoarding of Lord Krishna.She looked at that and thought she didn't want to live anymore. She told her mother she will kill herself as she couldn't bear this anymore.

Hours of standing, pain, physical, mental and verbal abuse … sitting like a frog which was a fun game for them. Only she and her friends knew how much pain it was to sit like that. She was in pain both in and out. Her mother got scared and held her in her lap. She cried and slept on her lap. She didn't have her dinner also.

In her mind for the first time she thought she should leave this place.

One night after the ragging sessions all of the students returned back to their rooms but Soumyadeep didn't return. Geet was not aware of that fact which she came to know the next day after she returned from college.

Geet's mom met his dad and he was crying to which her mom felt something was wrong. There was always a sense of fear prevalent over there as to what could happen next. Soumyadeep was taken behind the water tank where the bent iron pipes were there. Those dirty seniors made him bend down over those pipes and hit on his spine with their knuckles. Initially uncle thought no one has returned yet. When his dad noticed everyone came back except him and it was too late they started searching for him and found him lying unconscious over there with all bruises. Later he realised he was unconscious for more than 2 hours. Geet could not hold her tears realising what pain he must have gone through. She wished all these trash people should get double the pain what they have given everyone.

Next day something happened which shook her. Morning 4 am she heard a knock at her door. Both Geet and her mom were so scared they didn't even dare to ask who was there initially. Knowing that place had no security she and her mom were shivering. But as the knock continued Geet's mom asked who was it then some lady answered it's me. Both of them realised the voice was familiar and they hesitantly opened the door. Geet saw Joydeep's mom standing there and crying. Geet's heartbeat literally stopped and what happened she could not even think. Aunty came inside and started crying. Geet closed the door and turned on the light. Most of the time that city had no lights and powercut was an usual affair over there. Mom asked her what happened to which she answered Joydeep wanted to quit the course and go back home that day itself by morning flight. Geet and her mom were shocked to hear that. Aunty kept on telling he was not ready to listen to anyone. He was crying and yelling at everyone. Geet didn't want others to know about it. Aunty felt helpless so she came to Geet to speak to her once if she could talk to him. She immediately rushed to his room. He was sitting on the cot and crying looking all angry with a red face. Geet sat next to him and started talking to him. She told him "We all are there together. All of them were going through the same phase but we should not quit. This too shall pass." Probably he felt better after speaking to her and agreed to stay back. She came back to her room. She knew one thing deep down in her heart she too wanted the same thing.

Chapter Fourteen

College

Now coming to the college, it was an old building the usual old Government type. Nothing so glamorous just basic. The classrooms were all basic how every educational institute was. Classes with benches which could be shared with other batchmates. One blackboard with chalks for teaching. First year started with three basic but very important foundation subjects: Anatomy, Physiology, Biochemistry.

First class was Anatomy. One Mam came and she told everyone about the class schedule and mentioned about the books. A list was given. Since it was not a very developed place only three volumes of Cunningham were available at that time for purchase. Rest was yet to be bought. The first class of anatomy flew above her head. It was like a long jump from 12th standard to some ocean and she didn't know anything in between. She felt maybe everyone felt the same way like her. She opened the book for one time she got so scared seeing how difficult it was that she mastered the courage to flip through the pages.

Geet and her batchmates didn't have the freedom to walk around the college once they entered the premises. All those nasty seniors kept surrounding them like an armour not in the right sense. They didn't allow them to grab any food even if they were hungry. It was a jail or probably worse than that. After the first anatomy theory class they were asked to come to dissection hall for anatomy practical classes. Geet along with other 99 batchmates went to the hall. She saw two human bodies were kept for the purpose and they were asked to stand around the tables to see the dissection process. No specific numbers were allotted. It was a mess of 100 people flocking together around the tables trying to see the dissection process. She was sure no one saw anything other than the people who managed to be in the front or second to them. She tried to squeeze in and she heard something being discussed nothing of which really made sense to her. Being a new subject, she knew it would take a lot of effort and time to get hold of an entirely new branch.

After the class finished everyone went to wash their hands as they touched the specimen (deceased person) trying to understand the anatomy. During the entire class her eyes were continuously tearing up because of formalin being used for embalming the dead bodies. She didn't get scared at all seeing the dead bodies which her mother thought she would be quite terrified of. At the washing area there was no tap for washing. Few buckets with water and a soap bar was all that was over there to wash hands. Geet went to wash her hands and after she finished washing her hands she saw feet of a human being above her head to which she lifted her head and saw a dead person's leg being mounted probably for embalming purpose at a later time. Although Geet's mother thought her daughter was very coward as she used to scream seeing cockroaches luckily she didn't faint in the dissection hall and neither over the washing area. She got very scared at the washing area but didn't scream. She ran out of the place. Most of the times they never attended more than one class as most of the times they would be dragged to some other empty halls or places by seniors as soon as they stepped out of the class.

Geet had roll number 54 in the class probably in order of admission or maybe alphabets. They had one day of medical check up which was done in the OPD building over there. During that check up they were taken for blood tests, X ray and few ophthalmological evaluations. As she was waiting along with all other batchmates and seniors in front of the X-ray room to get her chest X ray done, one guy stepped over there and kept on speaking with the seniors. She was standing there waiting for her turn when that guy turned towards her and said "Oh so you are Geet. Waiting to meet you in the hostel". Geet was frozen for a moment knowing that it was not good. She was scared like hell. She understood one thing there is something wrong why that guy should wait for her in the hostel and how can guys come to girls hostel. She was so perplexed that she just wanted to go back to her room. She heard in flying words that guy was a resident in the Department of Radiology. She didn't believe that too because she didn't trust anyone over there if they were really what they looked. Geet started hearing stories about toppers turned into drug and alcohol addicts slogging for years unable to pass MBBS. One such guy was like the don of the hostel and he apparently was waiting to meet all juniors specially Geet.

She noticed the OPD building was so busy with people flocking like some market trying to get an OPD ticket. Wards were all very messy crowded with patients like you have never seen before.

The wards were inscribed with boards with the local language as well as in English indicating directions, wards, OPD. The wards were not very clean and it was just like a market. As one entered the college premises one could notice the college hall or the auditorium being used for different college functions, fresher's day and so on. Geet never got a chance to see the hall from inside. She just caught a glimpse of the hostel buildings which were very old with horrible maintenance. She didn't step inside the hostel till the day she came to shift all her stuff.

Now the lady senior gang made rules for all the juniors specially girls regarding the dress code. Now Geet decided to wear normal salwar suits for daily college as there was no uniform and she found it more comfortable and suitable for the college environment. Suparna and her lady group one night called up all of them after one of the ragging sessions got over and asked all of them to give them money whatever amount they asked them to pay. Geet's mom asked politely what was that money for to Suparna to which Suparna became furious. She ignored Geet's mom and told Geet "Can't you tell your mother to keep quiet?". She started addressing everyone in singulars. Geet was so mad at Suparna but she felt helpless like all others. She told everyone she is going to buy dresses for all girls and they have to wear the same dress to college.

So finally the dress came. Geet and her batchmates were shocked to see the dress. It was synthetic material violet saree whose cloth material was just the one used for puja pandals paired with a green blouse with similar material. Two ribbons of red and blue were given to tie their hair with two braids to be made on either side. One orange handkerchief to be attached on the saree with a pin. One pair of black rubber slippers usually used by the construction working persons was given to them. Literally all present over there were speechless.

How were they going to wear that and go to a medical college that too from Dharamsala crossing the entire city. Like her all others knew they had no option. Next day they all went to college with violet synthetic saree with green blouse, red ribbon flower on one braid and blue ribbon flower on another braid. She pinned the orange handkerchief on the saree on the left hand side. She wore her rubber slippers and went to college with her mom.

She took a rickshaw and went to college. Throughout her journey she noticed people staring at her and her batchmates. She just knew this was part of the journey and she didn't have options. Class started and she noticed though other batchmates belonging to other states had some dress codes their's was the worst. No one had such terrible dress. Once Mam came to the class she took attendance and when Geet and her batchmates were answering their calls, the teacher was laughing and then she commented "Oh ragging dress". Geet was furious at the fact that being a teacher how could she watch this and laugh. If she had some sense she would have enquired who made them wear such dress and she would have taken strict actions against them.

During one such day after they finished the class as they were about to exit they found a bunch of those nonsense people who dragged them to a big hall which was more like a gallery classroom. It was a huge classroom with wood furnishing. They were made to sit not on the bench but on the furnished ground on each steps. Geet sat alone on one step. They were given samosa to eat. The stage which was actually the classroom stage was used for ragging. That was the only day the entire 100 batchmates were sitting together for ragging. Geet started hearing speculations about students being drugged. She was so scared that she didn't eat the samosa. She crumbled it with her hands slowly moved towards the bench and threw the samosa below the bench without anyone's notice.

Boys were made to wear two coloured socks, white aprons being rolled above like blouse and trousers tucked inside the socks. For once Geet smiled a little watching them dance to "DOLA RE DOLA RE". They made random people propose each other. Though that day nothing much was happening still deep down in her heart she knew everything was not fine. As she stepped out of the auditorium she saw Sourav waiting outside behind the pillar for her. All her batchmates started pulling her leg but Geet didn't want to start the conversation and she quickly ran out of that place.

She actually was scared to come to college by then. The only safe place for her was her room.

Chapter Fifteen

Food

Food is a quintessential part of everyone's life specially for Geet. From the first day she had terrible problems in adjusting to the cuisine. She felt she was not the only one having food issues everyone was like her. Initially everybody would find problems but slowly everybody would adapt to it or find some alternatives. What shocked her was that there were hardly any proper restaurants to have food. As the place was shut down by 4 pm she like others hardly had time to go out and have something. By the time they returned back to Dharmasala they had to run to a nearby eatery to pack some dinner. There were few small fast food centres or some vegetarian meal places. Cleanliness was on the zero point. Still she and her mom managed to find one vegetarian meal place where they could pack some vegetarian meal and at least have something to eat. Though that place was half dark in smoke still the food was a little ok so it became their almost regular place to pack dinner. Night after all the ragging sessions were over it used to be 9 or 10 pm and as it was not a suitable place to go out she never dared to go out and look for food. She knew it would be of no use anyways since all shops shut down by 4 pm.

With time she understood her jobless seniors had no work other than ragging them, no classes, no attendance, no studies. So one fine day as all parents along with their kids were coming back all seniors on a rampant note started telling everyone to follow them. All started walking along with them and suddenly they saw themselves walking into some restaurant. Geet was thinking where were they going but she felt there was no point in even thinking as no one could even ask them. All sat and had their lunch. After lunch those nasty seniors asked all juniors to pay the bill which meant parents had to pay the bill.

Paying the bill was not a concern but at least once they should have told that "We are going for lunch". Like this many times they would take money for no reason and no one had the right to ask also. Actually no one dared in the fear that they would get beaten up.

Slowly like Geet everybody's health started deteriorating. Her mom realised even it was becoming difficult to stay like that for her also. She went to a nearby shop near to Dharamsala and bought a small click stove. She bought few utensils and some food stuff to cook. Athough it was not allowed to cook in Dharamsala her mom decided to cook or else they would die of hunger. She had to cook secretly without the hotel people knowing. She used to close the windows, door and cook. She went to the local market and to their surprise not a single man was there in the market. All women ran the market. In the market the ladies were so rude if anyone tried bargaining they used to raise their voice and show their chopping big knife to them. The market was filled with all fermented and dried fish. The smell was unbearable. Except few grocery shops everything was run by women. She grabbed few vegetables, oil, rice, dal. That's all they needed at that moment to feed themselves a meal. Geet's mom started making some boiled vegetables with rice at night. She used to cook basic food, no fancy meals. Few others started doing the same as there was no option. Somu's dad left and his mom stayed back. Somu's mom sometimes used to come and grab a meal with them. Somu's mom always treated Geet as her own daughter. Joydeep's mom used to always come and give her some food like she would do the same for her son. She was always grateful for that. They always used to come to her room and speak to Geet and her mom share their bad experiences but at the same time they felt better knowing they all were going through it together.

She came back one day from college and she was so sick mentally and physically. She told her mom she wanted to eat some good food. Her mom told her to go the opposite market and look for something good. She wanted to go but at the same time she was scared. She looked at the time and saw it was 4:30 pm and by 5:00 pm they would appear in Dharamsala. She was not sure if any shops would be open also. But her mom said just go and see. She just had 30 mins to go and come back. She didn't want them to see her outside. She ran without knowing much about the roads, traced one shop selling chowmein. Although she wished to sit and have it she didn't have options. She asked them to pack it and she rushed back to her room before they found her going out. She literally kept her heart in her hands because she knew if they saw her coming from outside she would have more terrible times during the ragging session. She felt so miserable that for food she had to be scared. What life she was leading actually made her sicker.

One day seniors didn't land up at Dharamsala. Geet guessed maybe they had exams. It was a sigh of relief for them. So after classes when they came back to Dharamsala, they all decided to go to the nearby market place and get some fresh air. All went with their parents. As always Somu and Joydeep along with their parents came together. Joydeep bought some chips packet and shared it with Geet. Geet bought few stuff and shared it with all. They smiled together some moments of happiness for them. They didn't speak about seniors at all as they knew that free time was precious and didn't want it to fade away.

She went one day with her mom to one local restaurant to have food and tried their meals. She found it difficult to have as it had lot of fermented food. Her mom told her you try cooking once you move to hostel as it would be healthier and you would be better with that food. She knew one thing everyone was having troubles with that food. She was preparing her mind to accept the fact that she had to stay alone within few days and manage everything including her mental status as she was all alone over there. It was scary for her not that her mom would not be there but thinking of the fact that she had no one to speak even in the ladies hostel.

Chapter Sixteen

Angels

Her angels Chanu aunty and Khamba uncle were angels in human disguise. She had no relation with them but what they did for her she could never forget. After uncle left, Khamba uncle used to always call and ask if they needed anything. He was also a busy person managing his business, family apart from being a National Football Referee but amidst all he never forgot them.

Inspite of his busy working times he never missed to call them a single day. He used to come and visit them whenever possible and asked them to come home whenever possible to have a meal with them. Gratitude towards him for everything could not be measured for what he did for them. Sometimes he brought fruits for Geet. She almost had tears in her eyes thinking of everything.

Chanu aunty was like her elder sister which she never had. She was an independent lady working with the state police department who was the sole bread earner for her family. She used to look after her old parents and also her brother's orphaned kids who were abandoned by their mother after their father's death. She was unmarried and gave up her life, dreams, happiness for everyone. Geet never saw anyone more selfless than her. (By the way she was also a National Football Referee and later she got selected by FIFA as an International Female Football Referee). She wished every lady was like her and could not even compare those nasty seniors of hers even closer to her. She was an inspiration for her how she excelled as a daughter, aunty, sister and also in her professional life. Inspite of everything so busy in her life she never forgot Geet and her mom. She considered Geet as her responsibility. She used to come whenever possible. She once came down and saw Geet not looking fine. She knew all was not right after hearing to all what was going on. She told them just tell me whenever it is too much I will see them personally. Geet knew she was into police and was a strong lady but didn't want to trouble her. If her seniors misbehaved with her they would mess up with the wrong person. Chanu aunty knew Geet loved fish so she told them she would come with food the next day. She didn't want to trouble her but Chanu aunty was adamant that she would bring food the next day.

Next day in the afternoon she came with a big box with lots of food. She asked Geet to open the food container with multiple small steel containers stacked one on another. She opened and found vegetable curries, fries, dal, rice, fish. She asked her to start with the fish curry. She asked Chanu aunty to have food with them but she told them that she just had her lunch after her duty got over. Chanu aunty left home at morning 5:30 am for her duty. After a whole day of standing and working she went home had her meal and quickly came to Geet's place with the food. Geet knew Chanu aunty was not from a very affluent family but still she managed to get her so much food. Geet took the fish curry made with bamboo shoots with minimal spices as she knew Geet was not well and might not well tolerate spices. As Geet had her first morsel of food, tears rolled down her eyes just not because it was a home cooked meal so tasty cooked with so much love but thinking how could she ever repay this kind lady. Did really God exist in humans then she saw that already. She had never tasted anything like that. She was happy to have that meal. Chanu aunty left them with the food as she had to get back home for some work. Geet had lots of food left for night also. She and her mom had a happy sleep.

Geet and her mom decided to pay a visit to Chanu aunty's home one day when seniors had exams and decided not to come for their ragging sessions. Chanu aunty had asked them to come home couple of times for a meal but Geet and her mom refused as they didn't want to trouble them anymore. Her home was not very far from the college. She informed Chanu aunty that they would be coming to pay her a visit. She bought sweets for her family and took a rickshaw with her mom.

They reached her home after little enquiry from a nearby shop. She was greeted by Chanu aunty's family. She sat on the corridor of the house along with Chanu aunty's parents. It was a very basic house which actually needed renovation but probably it was difficult for them due to their financial constraints. For a moment Geet thought this lady had so much problems but she never showed that on her face. She faced everything all alone as she had no one to help her. They offered Geet sweets, tea and some snacks. They asked her to stay for some food but they refused. She had a fresh breath of air in their house. Around the house she noticed so much greenery with lot of trees. Their gate was also not in proper shape. She held her tears seeing what conditions they were living in with a single person's income. Still she smiled and helped people no matter how less she had in her store. Geet learnt kindness from her and how precious it was to people like her. She wished someday she could be of some help to her. She also met her deceased brother's beautiful daughter Liklai and son who were equally sweet like her. Geet and Liklai exchanged numbers and spoke for quite sometime.

Before leaving they said goodbye to everyone and her whole family asked them to come again with more time and probably for a meal. Chanu aunty came till the main road till they got into a vehicle. She showed a small snacks shop which was run by one of her aunties near to her house. She told them all her seniors come over there to have evening snacks. She also told Geet she recognised few of them very well as they have been coming here for years and even they recognised her well as she used to come to Dharamsala to visit her. One thing her seniors had the biggest problem with Geet was her local connections which they didn't like. Chanu aunty told Geet if they crossed any more lines she could teach them their lesson as she was a strong police lady but Geet refused as she didn't want her to get into trouble because of her. They left early as that city was not safe and everything would shut down soon.

Geet wanted to go out for a meal with Chanu aunty but it never happened due to the mismatch of timings between her college and aunty's duties. For one thing she learnt kindness can change everything and the world would be a better place if more people like her existed.

Chapter Seventeen

Sentinel

Geet and her batchmates were tired of the daily ragging sessions and it was more than 10 days all these were going on the same abuse, beating, torture. They were all sad but they knew they had no options. 5 days of seat surrender was also over now what could they do.

Her great seniors informed them that they a regional association by the name "SENTINEL" which was managed by them and included only people of their ethnicity and their state.

What their real purpose was only God knew but as they said it was to help students to which she laughed in her mind. Help? Really? …… Beating students that is what help is?. Extortion, harassment, beating, ill behaviour was all they were offering in real sense. This was probably the last few days in Dharmasala for all of them. The boys were already being allotted hostels and they would be moving out soon.

"SENTINEL" party was scheduled by some seniors on one such evening and for that they took money from all juniors. Everyone paid the amount without knowing for what it was. They were asked to prepare for the party. So the night before all her batchmates went to the rooftop to discuss about next day's event.

It was pitch black darkness except from the light coming from the rooms. She sat with Joydeep and Somu near the water tank. She saw the moon with a nearby tall building which looked a little on the expensive side with glass covering the building. She saw two men with big guns walking in the building and probably some military dress which she could not make out properly. Not only she, Somu and Joydeep also saw the same. They were scared and they decided to leave fast. They left quickly in half bent position. Geet rushed to her room and informed her mom of the same. Her mom was also scared then.

Her room was on the outer aspect of Dharamsala facing the market. She started hearing stories of a lady's mysterious death which happened over there few months ago. Some said it was a blast while others quoted some other reason. It was the same area where Geet's room was there and she wondered what would happen if something like that happened again.

She also heard that because of the political turmoil the administration hardly functioned and it was the orders of the local goons whose orders supervened. Even most of the TV channels were not allowed to be broadcasted other than few local channels. It was as if the rest of the country was disconnected from them.

Sentinel party started the next day after classes. A mat was spread on the 5th floor of Dharamsala. All seniors sat on one side and juniors sat on one side. In order all were called to introduce themselves. They expected all to introduce in their local slang but as Geet didn't know that she introduced herself in her usual way in very few words as quick she could to run away from there. Few people sang songs including Sangeeta. Few seniors spoke in order of their self-proclaimed designations in the Association as Secretary, President and so on. She just wanted it to get over and get back to her mom. After their nonsense talks got over they handed some food packets with some sweets and snacks which Geet didn't touch and took it to her room to share it with her mom.

The next day all the boys got hostel allotment and it was their last day at Dharamsala. Geet was sad as she would not meet Somu and Joydeep so frequently now. Everyone came out on the corridors and were enjoying their last day together. She saw Joydeep near her room and started speaking to him. He asked her if she was planning to leave the college. Geet was shocked as to how he could read her mind. She just smiled faintly and she guessed he got his answer. He told her to leave this place as early as possible because her name was number one in the list in the boy's hostel. This made her scared but made no sense to her. "How could she be in the boy's hostel?". Suddenly she saw Sangeeta's mom in one corner and listening to everything. She pretended to have not seen her mom and wondered how terrible people could be. She realised people like her were the reason for making life more horrible for others.

They were informed that once all moved to hostel they would have a formal freshers party for the entire batch.

Next day Khamba uncle came to meet Geet. He helped Geet buy some chocolates. She went and gave chocolates to everyone and bid them goodbye. When she went to Akash's room she saw him sitting on the cot trying to pair his nails. Aunty started telling he has never done this in his entire life as aunty used to do it for him. Akash replied "I am trying to learn as mom would be leaving today". Geet felt very sad and she gave him the chocolate and said good bye to him too. She was actually scared of the fact that now these people were going to have a greater population of seniors in the hostel. What happens next will be a disaster that much was very clear to her.

Chapter Eighteen

Departure

Now as the boys moved to the hostel, it was turn for the girls to move to hostel too. They were asked to come to hostel for shifting in the evening after classes. Geet went back to Dharamsala after classes. She along with her mom found out one shop where she could buy all household stuff.

Her mom bought her pillow, quilt, pullovers, water tank, cooking utensils, pressure cooker and many more. Whatever she could remember of she bought from the shop. The shopkeeper was very friendly and helpful. He guided them what all they should buy as he was well acquainted with that place. He was a non local but knew the place very well as he was settled over there for many years.

Geet and her mom put everything in a vehicle and moved towards the hostel. As they reached the hostel they saw all the boys (seniors) flocking near the girl's hostel. Geet wondered what these nonsense people were doing over there. She was informed to stay in the P.G Hostel as there were no rooms available in the main hostel. How much truth was there in that God knew. She had to share her room with one of her batchmate. She was given the room number.

There was no security at the entrance. She entered the room and was speechless at the sight of the room.

It was a tiny room with two basic cots with dirt filled beddings. Spider cob webs filled up the room. She was sure that this room was not cleaned for months. Geet saw her roommate didn't arrive till then and there was no luggage kept inside the room. Geet selected one bed next to the window. The bedding was so dirty even if someone patted on it one big dust storm would arise.

The walls were covered with all cards which probably belonged to previous senior's and who never bothered to even clean it. She wondered how she stayed in this room with such terrible dirt.

The floor was dirty as hell and there was water clogging on the floor at places till ankle length. She wondered if humans really stayed at that place. As soon as she opened the bathroom which was attached to the room she was about to vomit. Government bathrooms were at times cleaner than that. Her focus very quickly moved from the dirty bathroom to something else. She saw a huge tree with roots inside the bathroom which had cracked the walls of the bathroom. She stood there thinking if it was a place for a living or a forest. She for sometime looked at her mom who was even shocked to see all that. More than her it affected her mom. Geet knew one thing she had to clean everything before moving over there completely. Water was clogged inside the bathroom above ankle level. The fan blades could not be seen due to dirt and cobwebs. Geet could not take back the stuff. She somehow managed to keep her things. As there was no lock available she locked the room with her own lock. As they were leaving seniors started calling her towards the opposite side hostel. They asked her to come inside. She wondered how could boys go so freely inside ladies hostel. Her mom moved along with her from the main gate of the hostel to the main hostel. There was a big area as one entered inside the hostel where it was filled with guys and next to it were all rooms. All the girls were roaming there few indecently dressed. There was a bench on which few of the guys were sitting and swinging their legs. All the guys were freely going inside the rooms. Geet wondered what was happening and if it really was a ladies hostel. No security nothing it was like a free birds entrance. Her mom was waiting at the entrance of the main hostel and watched everything silently. Geet saw few seniors coming out of their rooms cracking jokes with the guys. Suddenly she saw Sampa stepping out of one room. She called Geet and asked her to come to one room. She caught one glimpse of Suparna also. Sampa took her to one room where there were many girls including Suparna. All of them were looking at her as if they would eat her up.

Sampa introduced Geet and then one of them said "So this is Geet?"

Geet was shivering as she was scared anything could happen over there. Later when she came outside her mom told her even she was scared as they took her inside. Sampa and others started saying … "Come to hostel fast we will see you there". Geet asked permission if she could go. Suparna had a terrible smile and told her rudely "Go". "We will see you in the hostel". Geet knew very well what all that meant. She quickly rushed out of the hostel.

As soon as she came out she saw Sourav at the gate. He started talking to mom and asked her when is Geet going to shift to hostel. Mom replied politely that she was very homesick so she would like to keep Geet with her till she left. He was pretending to be so kind and replied "Aunty keep her with you till you are there she might feel better. Anyways after that she has to live with us only."

What did that "us" mean?

Geet's mom greeted Sourav and quickly rushed towards the maingate. Before Geet spoke her mom said "You are going back home. I don't want my daughter to become a doctor at the sake of giving herself". She understood what all happened in that hostel and anyone could come and go over there. No rules no one to complaint. Before she left she saw a short lady wearing jeans and a tee stepping out of the hostel while someone was telling loudly she is the warden. Geet's mom did not see her but Geet saw her. That lady kept on making signs to Geet not to turn her mother and show her. She thought what was wrong with that lady or was it because she was also equally involved in all of these and didn't want to be questioned. Geet thought what a terrible lady she was. All these made her mind more stern to leave the place.

As she reached home Geet told her mom she too didn't want to continue and she thought about it for long time. Mom called Geet's dad and told him everything. She told him about her decision. He was completely against it. He was staying abroad and had no idea what was happening in his wildest dreams. He couldn't imagine Geet leaving everything with no clues about her career. He and mom had a heated conversation. He told them to stay over there and he would come over there within a week. Mom told him she didn't want to lose her daughter and she won't wait. All her dad wanted her to become a doctor but her mom having experienced it knew what it would be leaving Geet over there. Either she would die or something terrible would happen. She called up uncle and explained everything. He agreed to mom and told her to let him know if any help was needed. He told mom to contact Khamba uncle for any urgent help. Slowly Geet came to know about mysterious deaths in the hostel, stories of molestation, torture which made her sterner regarding her decision.

Now the festival time was coming in about two months. Since the college was giving a monthly stipend along with travel concessions, all students were getting the forms filled up and booking their flight tickets as the tickets would get very pricey later. Geet's mom told everyone her dad would be sending the tickets for her. She didn't want anyone to raise an eyebrow.

She came to know everyone's parents booked the tickets to get back home. Geet's mom discussed it with Somu's mother and Joydeep's parents. Both of them agreed to her decision as they were worried about a girl's safety. Except Somu and Joydeep's parents no one asked her mom about going back home. Rest all booked their tickets together but didn't even bother to ask Geet's mom even once. Even her mom didn't care about all these much. Geet's mom called up the travel agent and got two tickets for the same day travel as Joydeep's parents.

The next day Geet was not feeling well. She decided not to go to college. Her mom was scared of leaving her alone. So she turned off all the lights, fan and asked Geet to lie on the bed silently without making any noise. She closed all the windows and locked the room from outside. The previous day she went to the shop where they bought all her hostel stuff. The owner was very helpful. Mom told him briefly that she was planning to withdraw her daughter from the course as it was dangerous to leave her daughter over there. He even told her mom to leave this place as early as possible. Mom asked him if she could return the items she bought from his shop. He agreed to it and agreed to refund the money after minimal deductions.

After locking Geet in the room she went to the hostel. Luckily it was functional hours so classes were going on and there was no one in the hostel. She rented a vehicle moved out majority of the stuff except bedding stuff, water tank and few more. She brought them back to the shop and refunded them. She decided to leave the rest of the stuff in the hostel. While Geet was locked up in the room she heard few people coming and knocking on the windows but she kept quiet.

Few more incidents happened even before these hostel events that actually triggered Geet's mom to take the decision to take back her daughter. One day evening there was no power supply and Geet was lying on her bed as she was not feeling well. Sangeeta's mom and few more of her batchmates arranged a party for the seniors. Sangeeta was staying in the room next to Geet but neither Geet's mom nor she had any idea about this party. Both Geet and her mom didn't bother about it and everyone was called except Geet and her mom. Geet's mom kept the door open as it was very hot waiting if the power supply would resume soon. Suddenly she saw all her batchmates and a huge group of seniors flocking around Sangeeta's room. Both Geet and her mom didn't even bother to come out and see what was happening. Later Joydeep's mom told them it was a big party. Once they were leaving suddenly all the seniors rushed inside Geet's room. They were such indecent people they didn't have the courtesy to knock at least once or take permission before entering the room. Once they entered, Geet was in a dilemma for what they have come to this room. She got up and sat. They started asking her mom if she was planning to take away her daughter. Till then mom had no plans to take away Geet from that place. Even she was surprised who told them all this stuff. Mom asked who told them such rumours. They started threatening her mom. "Even if you are thinking like that you also know it better that you can't take your daughter even if you want". Geet was frozen upon hearing this. Her mom got so angry that she raised her voice and told them "Let me see who touches my daughter or dares to take her away". She also said it was her daughter and she had every right to do whatever she wished for her daughter and she didn't require permission for that. Geet's mom was so furious that she asked them who gave them such news ... Surpanakha or someone from this hostel. They understood they have messed up with the wrong person so they quickly left. She couldn't understand why all were behind her daughter just because she was harmless.

They also enquired before leaving as to why she didn't go to college that day. Geet's mom told them that she was not feeling well. In real sense she was not well she developed colitis and was on medications. Immediately Saurav started telling "You admit her in the hospital and you stay back in the hotel. We will look after her." It was very alarming for Geet and her mom as anything could happen there.

Geet spoke to Chanu aunty and met her one last time. She told her everything and she too agreed on her decision. She gave off few stuff to Khamba uncle and asked him to keep them as he could use them. Finally, the day came.

All parents left no one spoke to her mom not even once except Somu and Joydeep's mom. Akash's mom left few days prior to everyone. No one asked Geet's mom about tickets except them and all others booked their tickets together. Somu's mom left very early morning as she had an early morning flight. Joydeep's mom came and told them that they were leaving. She also asked them to leave after everyone left. They did the same.

Khamba uncle came and asked them to leave. What was surprising was that the hotel people were trying to block their way. Khamba uncle came to the front and let them go. The hotel people understood that messing with a localite could be dangerous. Khamba uncle hired an auto and asked the driver to follow his scooty. Finally they started. Geet and her mom reached the airport. They didn't have words to thank Khamba uncle for everything he did for them. On the way to the airport she saw a famous temple where few years back a great religious leader was shot dead. She wondered how the people over there actually lived in real life.

Geet had tears in her eyes as she bid him goodbye and promised to be in touch. Although she was leaving for good actually she was clueless as to what her future held in for her. After 19 days of torture she was finally leaving that place.

Chapter Nineteen

Final Exit

As they reached the airport she saw Joydeep's parents who waved at her and she smiled back. Everyone was shocked after seeing Geet along with her mom. No one expected her over there. Everyone was drinking tea over there and for a moment she felt as if everyone went into a pause state seeing Geet with her mom. Maybe they understood Geet was leaving permanently or maybe they were angry with her both of which didn't matter to her in anyways.

Both she and her mom were scared that they would miss the flight which would be a nightmare for them as they left quite late from the hotel. Luckily the flight was delayed and they could take the flight. Geet got tea for her mom as they waited for the final boarding call. Geet didn't speak to a single person except Joydeep's parents. Due to late check in they didn't get seats together which was ok for both Geet and her mom.

Boarding started and she found herself seated next to her hostel roommate's father. She had a window seat whereas uncle had an aisle seat. As soon as the flight started which was about an hour's duration he started asking her when is she going to come back to which she said she didn't decide. She replied politely whenever she felt better she would come back.

Then he started blabbering you didn't inform anyone that you are going home to which she just looked at him. What irritated her the most was when he started asking "You are leaving like that how is my daughter going to stay in the hostel? Your all stuffs are kept in the hostel room. Who is going to look after them?"

Now Geet lost her mind. She looked back at him and answered him "Did I ask your daughter to look after my stuff? If she has problems with my things kept in the room, please ask her to throw away my stuff". She was so angry with him she really wanted to shout but didn't want to sound rude. She just prayed the flight should land soon.

As they reached they collected their baggage. She didn't speak to a single parent except Joydeep's parents. As it was a bit late, uncle asked Geet and her mom to accompany them. They planned to take the bus journey to home the next day. They went to the city after an hour's journey as the airport was about 40 km from the city centre. They found a hotel and went inside that.

As Geet's mom was about to book one room for her and her daughter, uncle said "Geet is like our daughter. If you don't mind, please don't book a separate room; it's not safe for both ladies to stay alone. There are two beds in our room. It's just a matter of night. We both will share one bed. You both can share another bed". Geet couldn't believe what he said. Who would care for someone so much! Geet's mom still asked them that they should not be a problem for them. Uncle convinced them that it was fine for them. The hotel people agreed to it and charged extra for that. Geet's mom paid for that. Night they went out and had dinner together. They came back to room and slept off. They spoke for sometime and called it off a day.

Next day morning they checked out of the room and went to the bus stand. They took the bus to their hometown. It was a 7 to 8 hours journey. They had lunch together as the bus stopped at one place. They all were happy to find home cooked food at one small eatery. Geet noticed few of her other batchmate's parents but she didn't speak to them neither they spoke to her.

Geet reached her hometown and her uncles came to receive her. She thanked Joydeep's parents and they bid her goodbye. Geet finally came home by evening.

At night, Soumyadeep's dad called Geet and he was crying like hell. "My son is gone. He is missing". Geet felt the ground just slipped off her feet. Uncle requested her to come to a place. She rushed to the designated place with her mom and uncle. Uncle came over there he was crying. Geet asked "What happened?". Geet heard the whole story now.

After Geet left in the evening all the seniors came rushing to Dharamsala as they got the news from someone that Geet was planning to leave. They went back to hostel and started beating Soumyadeep and Joydeep like anything. They got the information from other parents and batchmates that these people helped her escape from there. They were beaten so badly that they ran away from the hostel. Soumyadeep called his father from a telephone booth and narrated the event. After that he couldn't reach them on phone. Uncle felt helpless and didn't know what to do. That's when he called Geet. He requested her to at least go to the state administration and let them know what was happening. Geet agreed and she went back home. She couldn't sleep the entire night thinking of the torture Joydeep and Somu went through because of her. She kept on crying thinking what state they might be in. She felt miserable thinking that she only made Joydeep stay back and now she ran off from there.

Next day she went to one of the state official's home. He and his wife both were very kind towards her. He told her that they should have called from there and informed the Health ministry about all that was happening. They could have helped in someway. Geet explained to him the situations and how going out was also a terrifying fact over there. He asked her to give an official letter with all the seniors name and he would make sure they were taken out of the college. By that time the anti-ragging law had come to action but just because of the pathetic college administration it was a daily affair over there. They didn't even bother what terrible consequences people were living with over there.

Geet thought for a long time and decided not to give the letter. Everybody might think she was mad but she decided not to give the letter. She was scared they might harm her family. Many of them were from her city and she was scared about her siblings. She felt terrible but maybe it was that time which made her restricted.

Chapter Twenty

Thereafter

Geet's father came home. Her parents had arguments almost daily regarding her decision to leave the course. He tried persuading her mom but she was adamant not to send back her daughter. He kept on telling if she bothered about her future. Geet's mom had only one thing to say "I don't want my daughter to become a doctor at the expense of losing herself". Having not seen anything he was not ready to accept what was happening.

One fine day he told Geet's mom that he is going to go and drop her back to college. Geet was sitting on the steps leading to the 1st floor in her house. Her mom became furious and started fighting with him. They ended in a terrible fight. Her dad kept on telling … "She is over sensitive and how long will you keep your daughter behind your shadow?" Geet just sat there watching them having terrible arguments. She felt miserable …… miserable and tears rolled down her eyes. No one understood what she was going through. People started telling her you must have done something wrong that's why you are the only one who left the college. She didn't have a college nor she was studying for anything. Nothing felt good to her. She had no plans neither any clues what was happening. She stopped speaking to anyone. All her friends went to college except her. She hid herself in her room.

Her dad booked flight tickets for the next day as he was worried about her attendance in classes. He didn't want her to get into trouble during exams due to attendance shortage. As she was living in a joint family she had lot of uncles with whom she was staying. At night her youngest uncle requested them to have dinner with them. There was a silence prevalent all around her. No one spoke anything. Food plates were being placed but it was absolute silence. There was no sound other than the cutlery sound in the dining hall. Geet sat with her plate. She didn't touch the plate. She kept on thinking what would happen to her if she returned. Tears kept on rolling down her eyes. Her uncle and aunty saw that. Although they were very young and never spoke on top of her father, this time they couldn't keep quiet. Uncle said the first word "Please brother we won't let you take her back. This is not right". Aunty too joined uncle. Her mom started sobbing. Geet burst into tears. Uncle and aunty felt terrible looking at Geet and convinced her dad. Geet's father still tried telling if it is for money I will go and speak to them personally. "I will pay them 4 or 5 lakhs and ask them not to trouble my daughter". Geet's uncle was speechless by then and aunty started speaking then.

She told Geet's father "What are you talking about? You are just showing the lion more flesh to devour on." After lot of discussions he finally cancelled the tickets.

Geet came back from college that news no one knew except her family members and two of her closest friends. She didn't go out anywhere. But within few days the news spread. Geet's second youngest uncle came back from office and he came to Geet's room. He had a newspaper in his hand which was given to him by his colleague. It was a local newspaper in which it was mentioned in one of the news columns that one female medical student ran from the college due to ragging from that college. Her name was not given luckily. Uncle's colleague showed him the news and asked him if it was his niece as he knew she went to the same college to study. Uncle boldly denied the news. Geet was shocked as to how this news came out. Geet received one call from Sangeeta and Akash as to when she was coming back. She told them she would come back soon. She knew it was the seniors who made them call to enquire.

But the news didn't hide for long. One day afternoon some officials came to her home. They asked her dad if it was Geet's home. Her dad replied yes. They introduced themselves as officials from The Health Ministry. They asked if Geet was at home to which her dad could not lie and replied yes. They asked them to come with them to the Ministry Office. They told Geet's dad that they received an email from the college that a particular student was missing from the hostel and also was not present in the college. It became a big issue since she left without any notice. Geet and her parents went with them to The Health Ministry Office. She saw The Health Minister sitting over there along with other officials. They started bombarding questions at her why did she leave the college and that too without any notice. Geet's dad explained everything to them in details. The officials asked her why she didn't inform them about all these then they would have taken action by then.

Since the State Government was paying for her seat all they bothered was in loss and profit. Geet's dad got upset and told them clearly how did they expect someone to inform them from such a horrible place where anything could happen. "Do you expect my daughter to be alive if she would have done so?". They understood her situation but tried persuading her to go back. She sat quiet with tears rolling down her cheeks.

They gave contact details of one local professor over there whom she could contact anytime if problems arose over there. Even they told her she could visit him at his home if she wanted to. "He will take care of you." Geet's dad looked at the official and asked "Who will give protection in the hostel? There is no security guard nothing anyone can come and go that time who will give her security." The whole room became silent as they knew the bitter truth. Still they told her to think about it. She left the office along with her parents.

Few days later she received an official letter from the Ministry regarding the same and asked her to think again regarding joining back the college. She thought about it a lot. Finally, she went one day to the Ministry Office and gave her official resignation letter stating the reason being inhuman ragging practices.

She kept on crying while coming back thinking what's next. She joined graduation in a nearby college till she figured out what is to be done next. She visited Somu once when he came back home as his mother was not well after knowing about the terrible torture he faced over there. Aunty was bedridden but as soon as she saw Geet she gave her hand to her. She couldn't speak much just tears rolled down her eyes. She saw Somu sitting in one corner. She couldn't look at him. He had bruises all over with all marks on his face and neck caused by the beatings he got. She had tears in her eyes but didn't know what to say. She just placed her hand on his shoulder and told him everything would be ok to which he nodded his head. Somu's dad asked her to leave quietly as there were lot of people near their house who were studying in the same college. If they found out that Geet was visiting him then things would become more difficult for him. Joydeep's mother came and visited her sometimes. Even she went and saw them once. Aunty knew she loved Maggi and made her a big bowl of Maggi during her visit. She felt how grateful she was to have met such people. After a year she got into a medical college again and life changed for her after that day. She found a new family (friends) over there. She went to a new place, adapted to a new culture. She kept in touch with Somu and Joydeep through online messages. In her new college her roll number was 19. The number 19 became synonymous with her. The only thing she knew she could only escape because they didn't take her original documents from her which is usually not the case.

She learnt one thing amidst all that happened.

"Life is not a bed of roses.

But it's not full of pauses."

She continued her studies and at many times she was being questioned as to why she had those gap in years. She didn't want to explain everyone what all happened. At one point of time she stopped answering.

In the whole story her favourite part was Uncle's encounter with Shyamrup after a decade. Uncle was travelling by a bus to some distant place. He suddenly saw Shyamrup. Maybe Shyamrup didn't recognise him but uncle remembered all the nasty things he did to his niece. He just went near to his seat and guess what happened next. One big slap on his cheek. Suddenly all the bus passengers became furious and came to uncle as to why he did that. Then uncle started telling them in short how he used to rag people, torture them and make their lives miserable. Also, he told everyone what all Shyamrup did to his niece. Listening to the story all passengers started hitting Shyamrup. Shyamrup started screaming "Leave me. I am sorry. I didn't do anything". He somehow picked up his glasses and ran out of the bus. He ran away for his life. Geet's mom called her and told her about the incident. She never felt happier than this not because he was beaten up but for the fact that he realised what is pain which he gave everyone every day.

At the end she had one question…

Could anyone bring her back those lost years?

She knew the answer was "No".